Bossing Spreadsheets

A Girl's Guide to Data Analysis

While every precaution has been taken in the preparation of this book, the publisher assumes no responsibility for errors or omissions, or for damages resulting from the use of the information contained herein.

BOSSING SPREADSHEETS: A GIRL'S GUIDE TO DATA ANALYSIS

First edition. February 13, 2023.

Copyright © 2023 Sophie Johnson.

ISBN: 979-8215269671

Written by Sophie Johnson.

Dedicated to all the young women breaking barriers and taking the business world by storm. This book is for you, the ones who embrace challenges and know that data is the key to unlocking success. May it help you become the spreadsheet queen you were meant to be!

Introduction: Understanding the Basics of Spreadsheets

SOPHIE JOHNSON

Welcome to "Bossing Spreadsheets: A Girl's Guide to Data Analysis"! This book is designed for young business women who are looking to improve their skills and excel in their daily work life. Whether you're working in a company or running your own business, spreadsheets are a powerful tool that can help you streamline your work and make data-driven decisions.

BOSSING SPREADSHEETS: A GIRL'S GUIDE TO DATA ANALYSIS

In this book, we'll take a step-by-step approach to mastering spreadsheets, so you can become sheet savvy and excel in your daily work life. We'll start with the basics of creating and editing a spreadsheet, including how to input data, format cells, and use simple formulas. We'll also cover some key features of Excel and Google Spreadsheets, such as auto-fill and conditional formatting, that can save you time and make your data look more presentable.

We will also learn about more advanced topics such as data visualization, collaboration and sharing, and automation of tasks. We will also have a chapter dedicated to real-life scenarios to help you apply your skills in practice. By the end of this book, you'll have a solid foundation in spreadsheet basics and be ready to take your skills to the next level.

The book is divided into 10 chapters, each dedicated to a specific topic. Each chapter will have examples, exercises, and real-life scenarios that will help you better understand and apply the concepts covered. The book also includes screenshots and images to illustrate key concepts and make it more visually appealing.

Before we dive into the details, let's start by understanding the basics of spreadsheets. A spreadsheet is a document made up of rows and columns that can be used to organize and analyze data. Excel and Google Spreadsheets are two of the most popular spreadsheet programs available. They are very similar in functionality and interface but have some key differences. In this book, we will focus on Excel and Google Spreadsheets, but most of the concepts covered can be applied to other spreadsheet programs as well.

Now that you have an idea of what to expect in this book, let's get started on our journey to mastering spreadsheets!

Setting Up Your Spreadsheet: Customizing the Interface and Saving Time

In this chapter, we'll learn how to set up your spreadsheet for optimal efficiency and ease of use. We'll start by customizing the interface and then move on to some time-saving tips and tricks. By the end of this chapter, you'll be able to navigate your spreadsheet with ease and save time while working on it.

I. Customizing the Interface

The interface in Excel and Google Sheets refers to the layout and design of the program, including the various tools and features that are available.

In Excel, the interface is divided into several main parts:

- **The Ribbon**: This is the topmost part of the interface, which contains tabs such as "Home," "Insert," "Data," and "Review." Each tab contains a set of related commands and tools.
- **The Formula Bar**: This is located just above the spreadsheet and is used to enter and edit formulas and cell contents.
- **The Worksheet**: This is the main area of the interface, where the spreadsheet is displayed. It is made up of rows and columns, and each intersection of a row and column is called a cell.
- **The Status Bar:** This is located at the bottom of the interface and provides information about the current sheet, such as the number of selected cells, the sum of selected cells, and the current mode (e.g. "Insert" or "Overwrite").

In Google Sheets, the interface is similar, it has a similar layout, with a toolbar at the top, a formula bar, and a spreadsheet area. Google Sheets has a slightly different layout, the navigation tabs are located on the left, and the tools and options are located on the right.

Both Excel and Google Sheets also have the ability to customize the interface to suit your needs, such as adjusting the column width, row height, and font size, or hiding and showing certain toolbars and panels.

In short, the interface in Excel and Google Sheets is the layout and design of the program, including the various tools and features that are available, and it allows you to navigate, customize and perform actions on the spreadsheet easily.

Customizing the ribbon in Excel

To customize the ribbon in Excel, go to **File > Options > Customize Ribbon**. From there, you can add or remove commands, create your own tabs, and even customize the quick access toolbar. This way you can have the commands you use most often right at your fingertips.

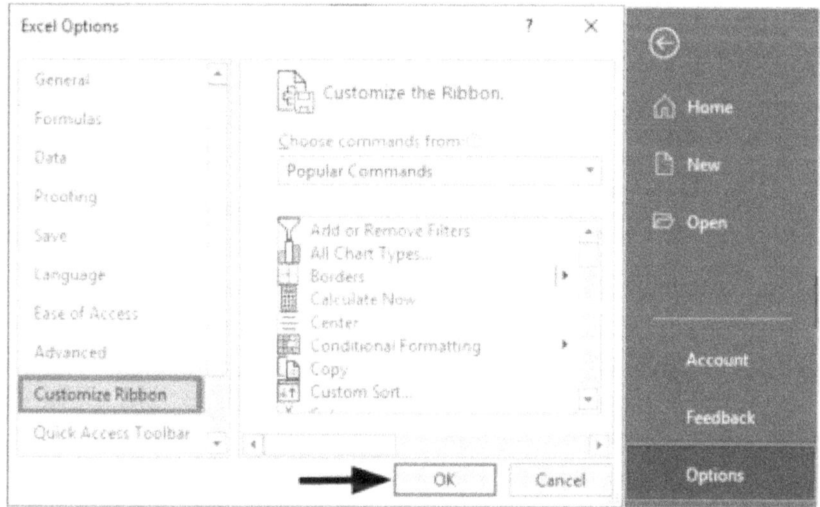

Figure 1 (Windows)

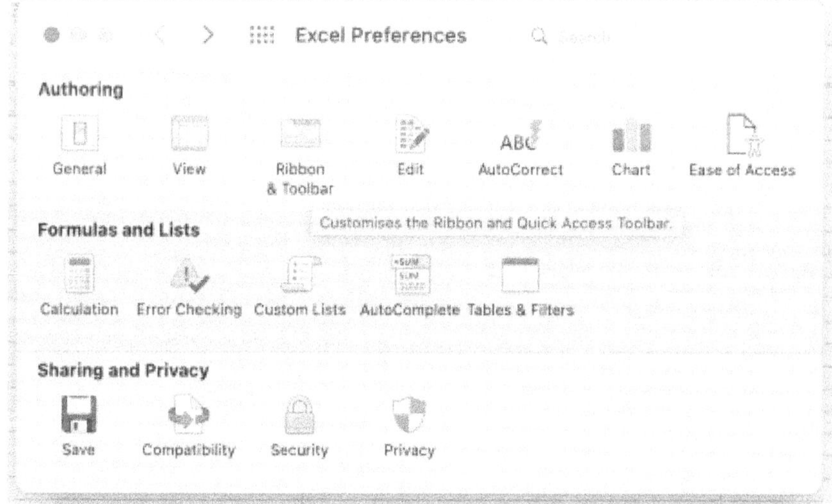

Figure 2 (MacOS)

II. Time-saving Tips and Tricks

Using keyboard shortcuts

Both Excel and Google Spreadsheets have a wide range of keyboard shortcuts that can save you time. For example, in both, you can use the shortcut "Ctrl + C" to copy, "Ctrl + V" to paste, and "Ctrl + Z" to undo.

Auto-fill

Auto-fill is another great feature that can save you time when entering data. Both Excel and Google Spreadsheets have an auto-fill feature that can automatically fill in data based on the pattern of the data you have entered. For example, if you want to enter a series of numbers, you can enter the first two numbers, then select them, and drag the fill handle to fill in the rest of the series.

Using conditional formatting

Conditional formatting is a powerful tool for identifying trends or outliers in your data. You can use this feature to format cells based on their content or value. In Excel, you can access the conditional formatting feature by going to Home > Styles > Conditional Formatting. In Google Spreadsheets, you can access it by going to Format > Conditional formatting.

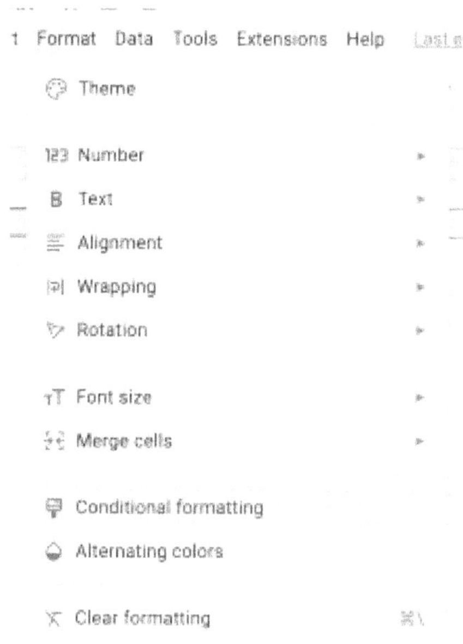

Using templates

Both Excel and Google Spreadsheets have a wide range of templates that you can use to quickly create a new spreadsheet. Templates include budget spreadsheets, invoices, calendars, and more.

By customizing your interface, using keyboard shortcuts, and taking advantage of other time-saving features, you'll be able to work more efficiently and effectively with your spreadsheets.

Organizing and Formatting Data: Tips and Tricks

In this chapter, we're going to take your spreadsheet game to the next level. We'll be diving into the nitty-gritty of organizing and formatting data like a boss. From sorting and filtering to formatting and styling, we'll cover everything you need to know to make your spreadsheets look and function like a pro.

Get ready to impress your colleagues and boss with your mad spreadsheet skills.

I. Sorting and Filtering Data

Sorting data in Excel

To sort data in Excel, go to the Data tab and select Sort. From there, you can choose to sort by one or multiple columns, in ascending or descending order.

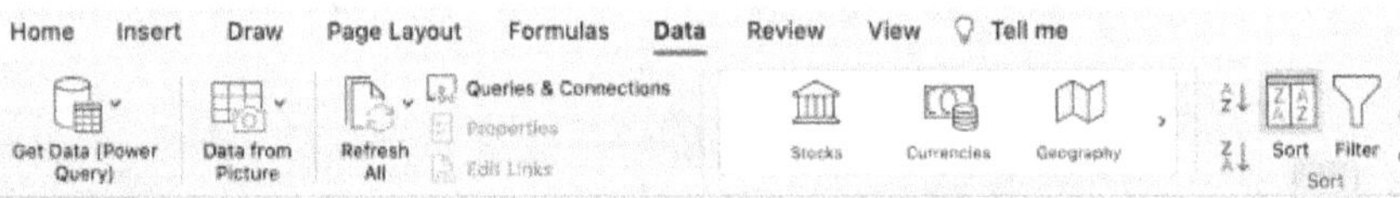

Filtering data in Excel

To filter data in Excel, go to the Data tab and select Filter. From there, you can choose to filter by one or multiple columns and specify the criteria for the filter.

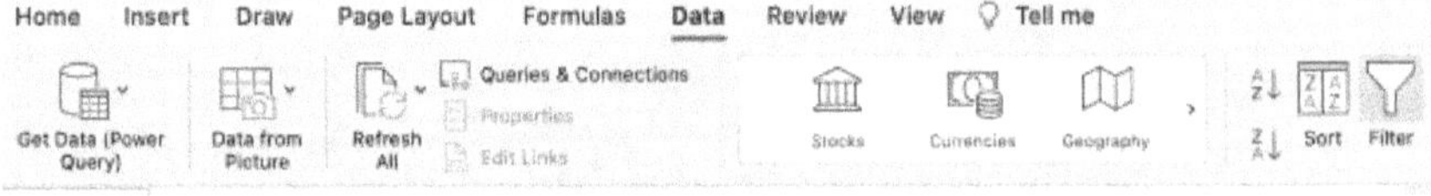

Sorting and filtering data in Google Spreadsheets

- To sort data in Google Spreadsheets, go to the Data menu and select Sort sheet by column. From there, you can choose to sort by one or multiple columns, in ascending or descending order.
- To filter data in Google Spreadsheets, go to the Data menu and select Filter. From there, you can choose to filter by one or multiple columns and specify the criteria for the filter.

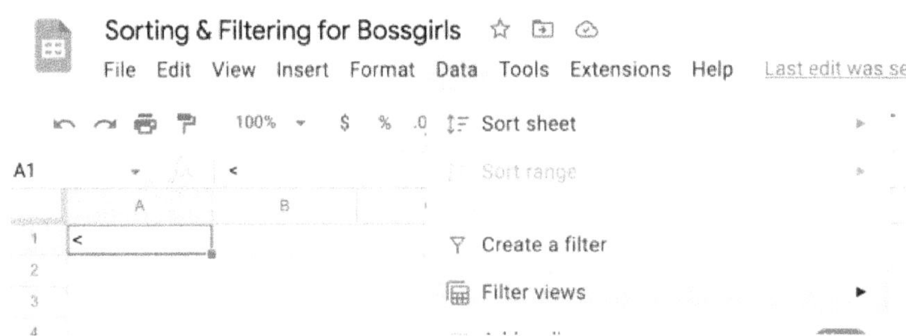
Sorting & Filtering for Bossgirls
File   Edit   View   Insert   Format   Data   Tools   Extensions   Help   Last edit was se
100% $ %   .0   Sort sheet
A1   <   Sort range
       A   B
1   <
2   Create a filter
3   Filter views
4

II. Formatting and Styling Data

Formatting and styling data in Excel and Google Sheets refers to the process of changing the appearance of the data in a spreadsheet, such as font type, font size, font color, cell background color, and cell alignment.

In Excel, formatting and styling data can be done using the Ribbon, which contains the Home tab, where you will find the commands for formatting and styling data. You can use the formatting options such as font type, font size, font color, cell background color, and cell alignment. You can also use the conditional formatting feature to automatically format cells based on their values or the values of other cells.

In Google Sheets, the process of formatting and styling data is similar to Excel. You can use the toolbar at the top of the interface to format text, cells, and sheets. You can also use the conditional formatting feature to automatically format cells based on their values or the values of other cells.

Both Excel and Google Sheets also have a wide range of options for formatting and styling data, such as custom number formats, cell borders, and data validation. You can also use the pre-built styles or create your own styles to make your data more visually appealing.

In short, formatting and styling data in Excel and Google Sheets is the process of changing the appearance of the data in a spreadsheet, such as font type, font size, font color, cell background color, and cell alignment, it allows you to make your data more visually appealing and easy to read.

. . . .

Formatting cells in Excel

To format cells in Excel, go to the Home tab and select the desired formatting options. You can change the font, font size, font color, and more.

Styling cells in Excel

To style cells in Excel, go to the Home tab and select the desired style options. You can choose from pre-designed styles or create your own custom styles.

Formatting and styling cells in Google Spreadsheets

To format and style cells in Google Spreadsheets, go to the Format menu and select the desired options. You can change the font, font size, font color, and more.

III. Conditional Formatting

Conditional formatting in Excel and Google Sheets is a feature that allows you to automatically format cells based on their values or the values of other cells. This is useful for highlighting important information, such as data that is above or below a certain threshold, or for identifying patterns or trends in your data.

In Excel, you can use conditional formatting to format cells based on a set of rules or conditions. For example, you can format cells that contain a value greater than a certain number, or cells that contain a specific text. You can also use conditional formatting to create data bars, color scales, and icon sets that visually represent data in a cell.

In Google Sheets, conditional formatting is similar, it allows you to format cells based on a set of rules or conditions. You can use it to format cells based on their values, or based on the values of other cells. Google Sheets also has a "Formatting rules" option, which allows you to set custom rules and conditions for formatting.

Both Excel and Google Sheets allow you to apply multiple conditions and multiple formatting styles to the same cells, this allows you to highlight multiple aspects of your data at once.

In short, Conditional formatting is a powerful feature in Excel and Google Sheets that allows you to automatically format cells based on their values or the values of other cells, it helps you to highlight important information, such as data that is above or below a certain threshold, or for identifying patterns or trends in your data.

Conditional formatting in Excel

To use conditional formatting in Excel, go to Home > Styles > Conditional Formatting. From there, you can set up rules to format cells based on their content or value.

Conditional formatting in Google Spreadsheets

To use conditional formatting in Google Spreadsheets, go to Format > Conditional formatting. From there, you can set up rules to format cells based on their content or value.

• • • •

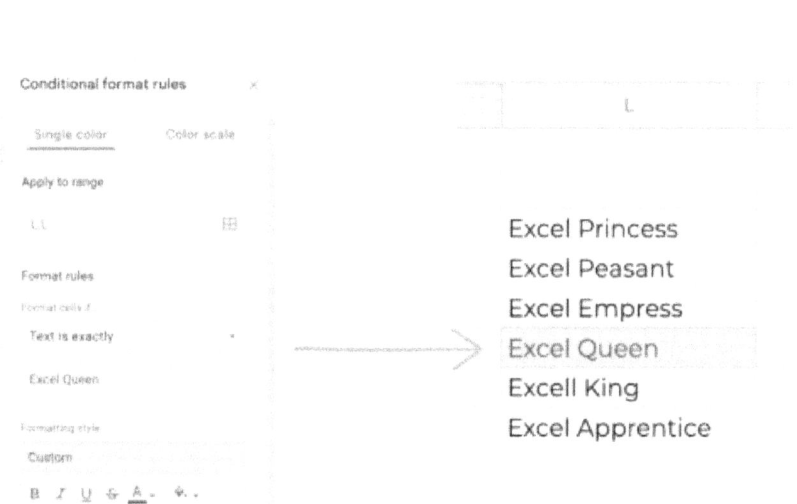

By mastering the art of sorting, filtering, formatting and styling your data, you'll be able to turn a chaotic spreadsheet into a well-organized, easy-to-read masterpiece. Not to mention, you'll be able to quickly identify trends or outliers in your data with conditional formatting. With the knowledge you've gained in this chapter, you'll be able to work more efficiently and effectively with your spreadsheets.

Formulas and Functions: Unleashing the Power of Excel and Google Spreadsheets

In this chapter, we're going to explore the powerful world of formulas and functions. Whether you're a beginner or an advanced user, you'll learn how to use these tools to perform calculations, analyze data, and automate repetitive tasks. By the end of this chapter, you'll be able to harness the full power of Excel and Google Spreadsheets to take your data analysis to the next level.

I. Getting Started with Formulas

Creating a formula in Excel

To create a formula in Excel, start by typing an equal sign (=) in the cell where you want to enter the formula. Next, enter the appropriate function or operator. For example, to add two cells together, you would enter =A1+B1.

Creating a formula in Google Spreadsheets

To create a formula in Google Spreadsheets, start by typing an equal sign (=) in the cell where you want to enter the formula. Next, enter the appropriate function or operator. For example, to add two cells together, you would enter =A1+B1.

II. Common Excel Functions

SUM function

The SUM function allows you to add up a range of cells. For example, to add up the values in cells A1 through A5, you would enter =SUM(A1:A5).

AVERAGE function

The AVERAGE function allows you to calculate the average of a range of cells. For example, to calculate the average of the values in cells A1 through A5, you would enter =AVERAGE(A1:A5).

COUNT function

The COUNT function allows you to count the number of cells in a range that contain numbers. For example, to count the number of cells in range A1:A5 that contain numbers, you would enter =COUNT(A1:A5).

III. Common Google Spreadsheets Functions

SUM function

The SUM function in Google Spreadsheets works the same way as in Excel, it allows you to add up a range of cells. For example, to add up the values in cells A1 through A5, you would enter =SUM(A1:A5).

AVERAGE function

The AVERAGE function in Google Spreadsheets works the same way as in Excel, it allows you to calculate the average of a range of cells. For example, to calculate the average of the values in cells A1 through A5, you would enter =AVERAGE(A1:A5).

COUNT function

The COUNT function in Google Spreadsheets works the same way as in Excel, it allows you to count the number of cells in a range that contain numbers. For example, to count the number of cells in range A1:A5 that contain numbers, you would enter =COUNT(A1:A5).

IV. Nesting Functions

Nesting functions in Excel

To nest functions in Excel, you can enter one function as an argument within another function. For example, to calculate the average of the sum of a range of cells, you would enter =AVERAGE(SUM(A1:A5)).

Nesting functions in Google Spreadsheets

Nesting functions in Google Spreadsheets works the same way as in Excel, you can enter one function as an argument within another function.

For example, to calculate the average of the sum of a range of cells, you would enter =AVERAGE(SUM(A1:A5)).

By mastering the art of formulas and functions, you'll be able to perform complex calculations, analyze data, and automate repetitive tasks in seconds. With the knowledge you've gained in this chapter, you'll be able to unlock the full power of Excel and Google Spreadsheets to take your data analysis to the next level and become an expert in your field.

Data Analysis and Visualization: Turning Your Data into Insights

In this section, you'll learn advanced spreadsheet techniques. We'll take a look at data analysis and visualization as an art form. You will learn how to visualize your data through the use of pivot tables and filters, as well as how to draw conclusions from it using charts and graphs. With the skills you've gained in this chapter, you'll be able to analyze and visualize data like an expert and take on any business challenge with confidence.

I. Creating Charts and Graphs

Creating charts and graphs in Excel and Google Sheets is important because it allows you to present your data in a way that is easy to understand and visually appealing. Charts and graphs can help you to identify patterns and trends in your data that might not be immediately obvious when looking at raw data.

Creating charts in Excel

In Excel, you can create a variety of different charts and graphs, such as bar charts, line charts, pie charts, and scatter plots. Each type of chart is suited to different types of data and can be used to highlight different aspects of your data. For example, a bar chart is a good choice for comparing the values of different categories, while a line chart is better suited for showing trends over time.

Creating graphs in Google Spreadsheets

In Google Sheets, the process of creating charts and graphs is similar, it allows you to create a variety of different charts and graphs, such as bar charts, line charts, pie charts, and scatter plots. Google Sheets also has a feature called "Explorer" which allows you to quickly create charts and explore your data with a few clicks.

Both Excel and Google Sheets also allow you to customize your charts and graphs, such as changing colors, adding labels, and adjusting the axis.

In short, creating charts and graphs in Excel and Google Sheets is important because it allows you to present your data in a way that is easy to understand and visually appealing, it helps you to identify patterns and trends in your data that might not be immediately obvious when looking at raw data, and it allows you to communicate complex information effectively.

II. Using Pivot Tables

Imagine you're a store manager and you have a big spreadsheet with all of your sales data. It has all the information you need, like the date of the sale, the item sold, and how much money you made. But it's hard to make sense of all that data, right?

Enter pivot tables! A pivot table is a tool that helps you organize and summarize all that data in a way that's easy to understand. Think of it like magic. You can "pivot" the data to see different perspectives, just like how a pivot on a door allows you to see both sides of a room.

Let's say you want to know which items are the most popular. With a pivot table, you can quickly and easily see which items have the highest sales. Or, maybe you want to know which day of the week is the busiest? With a pivot table, you can see that too!

It's like having a crystal ball that can show you all the insights you need to make important business decisions. It's not just for business either, it can be used to make sense of data in other fields too.

In short, pivot tables are your secret weapon to unlock insights from your data and make better decisions.

Creating pivot tables in Excel

Creating pivot tables in Excel is like being a superhero! You start off with a big spreadsheet full of data, just like a city full of people in need of help. But instead of saving people from burning buildings, you're going to save them from boring data!

First, you need to select the data you want to use for your pivot table. This is like choosing which part of the city you want to focus on - maybe it's just one neighborhood or maybe it's the whole city. Once you've selected your data, you'll go to the "Insert" tab and click on "Pivot Table." This is like putting on your superhero suit!

Next, you'll choose where you want to put your pivot table. This is like choosing where you want to set up your superhero headquarters. You can put it in a new sheet or an existing sheet.

Now, you get to start playing around with the data and see what kind of insights you can uncover. You'll drag different fields into the "Rows" and "Columns" sections, which is like going out and gathering information from different parts of the city. The "Values" section is where you'll put the data that you want to see, like crime statistics or population numbers.

Finally, you can add some finishing touches to your pivot table, like giving it a new name or changing the layout. This is like putting the finishing touches on your superhero headquarters.

And just like that, you've transformed boring data into valuable insights! You're a data superhero!

Creating pivot tables in Google Spreadsheets

To create a pivot table in Google Sheets, you can follow these steps:

◇ Open your Google Sheets document and select the range of cells that you want to include in the pivot table.

◇ Click on "Data" in the top menu, then select "Pivot Table." A new sheet will be created with a blank pivot table.

◇ In the right sidebar, you'll see a list of the columns in your data. These can be dragged and dropped into the "Rows" and "Columns" sections of the pivot table to group and organize your data.

◈ You can also drag and drop columns into the "Values" section to calculate things like sums and averages.

◈ Once you've set up the pivot table the way you want, you can use the options in the sidebar to further customize it, such as by sorting or filtering the data.

◈ You can also use the pivot table to create charts with the data.

It's important to remember to select the data range before creating a pivot table, as it won't work if you don't.

III. Using Filters

Filters are a way to quickly and easily sort through large amounts of data in a spreadsheet. They allow you to view specific rows of data based on certain criteria that you set.

In Excel and Google Sheets, you can apply filters to columns by clicking on the filter icon located in the header of the column. Once you click on it, a drop-down menu will appear with options to filter the data based on specific criteria, such as values that are greater than or less than a certain number, or text that contains or does not contain certain words.

You can also filter data based on multiple criteria at once. For example, you can filter a list of customers to only show those who live in a specific city and have made a purchase within a certain date range.

Filters can also be used in combination with other tools, such as pivot tables and charts, to more easily identify trends and patterns in your data.

In short, filters are a powerful tool that allows you to quickly find the data that is most relevant to you, whether you are looking to make a business decision, or just trying to organize your personal data.

Using filters in Excel

To use filters in Excel, go to the Data tab and select Filter. From there, you can specify the criteria for the filter and apply it to the data.

Using filters in Google Spreadsheets

Filters can be applied in Google Spreadsheets by selecting Filter from the Data menu. You can then apply the filter after defining its criteria.

BOSSING SPREADSHEETS: A GIRL'S GUIDE TO DATA ANALYSIS

Gaining proficiency in data analysis and visualization will allow you to derive valuable insights from your data and use them to guide your decision-making. Beautiful and useful charts and graphs are at your fingertips, as are pivot tables and filters for speedy data analysis. After reading this chapter, you should feel confident in your ability to analyze and visualize data, and you should be prepared to take on any business challenge.

IV. Additional Tips and Tricks

Customizing charts and graphs

To customize charts and graphs in Excel and Google Spreadsheets, you can use the formatting options available in the chart or graph editor. You can change the color, style, and layout of the chart or graph to make it more visually appealing.

Sharing and Collaborating

To share and collaborate on your spreadsheets in Excel and Google Spreadsheets, you can use the built-in sharing and collaboration features. You can share the spreadsheet with specific people or make it public, and you can also add comments and track changes to collaborate with others in real-time.

With this chapter, you're now a pro in data analysis and visualization. You'll be able to turn your data into insights that will help you make better decisions, and you'll be able to create charts and graphs that are both beautiful and informative. You're now ready to take on the business world like a boss. Remember, to always be curious and keep learning, you'll be surprised by how much you can achieve with this skill set.

Collaboration and Sharing: Working with Others on Spreadsheets

In this chapter, we're going to explore the world of collaboration and sharing on spreadsheets. Whether you're working on a team or just need to share your data with others, you'll learn how to use the built-in collaboration and sharing features in Excel and Google Spreadsheets. By the end of this chapter, you'll be able to collaborate and share your spreadsheets with others like a pro.

I. Sharing and Collaborating

Sharing and collaborating in Excel and Google Sheets are features that allow multiple people to access and edit a spreadsheet at the same time.

In Excel, you can share a spreadsheet by saving it to a shared network location or by sending it as an email attachment. You can also use Microsoft's OneDrive or SharePoint to collaborate on a spreadsheet in real-time.

In Google Sheets, sharing and collaboration are built-in features. You can share a spreadsheet by giving specific individuals access to the document, or by making it viewable or editable by anyone with a link. You can also set permissions to control who can view, edit, or comment on the spreadsheet.

When multiple people are editing a spreadsheet at the same time, Google Sheets will automatically merge the changes made by each person, and also allows you to see who made each change and when, this is called revision history.

Both Excel and Google Sheets also offer commenting and @mentioning feature, which allows users to leave comments and ask questions within the spreadsheet, making it easy to discuss and clarify information.

In short, sharing and collaborating in Excel and Google Sheets are great ways to work together on a project, whether you're in the same room or on opposite sides of the world, and it helps to keep track of the changes made by multiple parties and allows for easier communication.

Sharing a spreadsheet in Excel

To share a spreadsheet in Excel, you can use the built-in sharing feature. You can share the spreadsheet with specific people or make it public, and you can also add comments and track changes to collaborate with others in real-time.

Collaborating on a spreadsheet in Excel

To collaborate on a spreadsheet in Excel, you can use the built-in commenting and tracking changes feature. You can add comments to cells or specific ranges, and you can also track changes made by other users.

Sharing a spreadsheet in Google Spreadsheets

To share a spreadsheet in Google Spreadsheets, you can use the built-in sharing feature. You can share the spreadsheet with specific people or make it public, and you can also add comments and track changes to collaborate with others in real-time.

Collaborating on a spreadsheet in Google Spreadsheets

To collaborate on a spreadsheet in Google Spreadsheets, you can use the built-in commenting and tracking changes feature. You can add comments to cells or specific ranges, and you can also track changes made by other users.

III. Tips and Tricks

Setting permissions

To set permissions for shared spreadsheets in Excel and Google Spreadsheets, you can use the built-in permission settings. You can set different levels of access for different users, such as read-only or edit access.

Managing versions

To manage versions of a shared spreadsheet in Excel and Google Spreadsheets, you can use the built-in version management feature. You can view and restore previous versions of the spreadsheet, and you can also see who made specific changes.

By mastering the art of collaboration and sharing on spreadsheets, you'll be able to work effectively with others on your data. You'll be able to share your spreadsheets with others, and collaborate on them in real-time. With the knowledge you've gained in this chapter, you'll be able to work with others like a pro, and take your spreadsheet skills to the next level.

Automating Tasks: Using Macros and Scripts

In this chapter, we're going to delve into the world of automation. We'll learn how to use macros and scripts to automate repetitive tasks and save time. Whether you're working on a big project or just want to streamline your workflow, you'll learn how to use the built-in automation features in Excel and Google Spreadsheets. By the end of this chapter, you'll be able to automate tasks with ease and take your spreadsheet skills to the next level.

I. Macros in Excel

Macros in Excel are a way to automate repetitive tasks. A macro is a set of instructions that you can record and then play back later to repeat the same steps.

Macros are created by recording a series of steps that you perform in Excel, such as typing, formatting, or selecting data. Once you have recorded the macro, you can run it by clicking a button or using a keyboard shortcut.

Macros can be a powerful tool to automate repetitive tasks, such as formatting data or creating charts, and also can help you to simplify complex tasks. For example, you can use a macro to automatically format a large amount of data to a specific format, or to import data from a website into your spreadsheet.

Macros can be created using the macro recorder in Excel, which is an in-built tool, or you can use VBA(Visual Basic for Applications) to write the code of the macro. VBA is a programming language that is used to create macros, and it allows you to create more advanced macros that can interact with other programs and perform calculations.

In short, Macros in Excel are a way to automate repetitive tasks, saving you time and effort, and also help you to simplify complex tasks. It's like having a robot worker that knows how to do your Excel tasks for you.

Recording macros in Excel

To record a macro in Excel, go to the View tab and select Macros. From there, you can record your actions and save them as a macro for later use. This can include things like formatting cells, inputting data, or running calculations.

Running macros in Excel

To run a macro in Excel, go to the View tab and select Macros. From there, you can select the macro you want to run and click on the Run button. Once you've recorded a macro, you can run it at any time to repeat the actions you recorded.

II. Scripts in Google Spreadsheets

Writing scripts in Google Spreadsheets

To write a script in Google Spreadsheets, go to the Tools menu and select Script editor. From there, you can write your script using JavaScript and save it for later use. JavaScript is a programming language that allows you to create instructions for a computer to follow. In the case of Google Spreadsheets, it allows you to automate tasks or perform calculations on your data.

Running scripts in Google Spreadsheets

To run a script in Google Spreadsheets, go to the Tools menu and select Script editor. From there, you can select the script you want to run and click on the Run button. Once you've written a script, you can run it at any time to automate tasks or perform calculations on your data.

III. Tips and Tricks

Automating data entry

To automate data entry in Excel and Google Spreadsheets, you can use macros or scripts to fill in cells or ranges with specific data. This can be helpful if you have a lot of data to input, or if you need to input the same data multiple times.

Automating data analysis

To automate data analysis in Excel and Google Spreadsheets, you can use macros or scripts to perform calculations or analyze data on a schedule. This can be helpful if you have a lot of data to analyze, or if you need to perform the same calculations multiple times.

By mastering the art of automation, you'll be able to save time and streamline your workflow. You'll be able to automate repetitive tasks, and take your spreadsheet skills to the next level. With the knowledge you've gained in this chapter, you'll be able to automate tasks with ease. Remember, automation is the key to efficiency, don't be afraid to use it and keep learning.

Advanced Tips and Tricks: Taking Your Skills to the Next Level

In this chapter, we're going to take your spreadsheet skills to the next level. We'll explore advanced tips and tricks that will help you work more efficiently and effectively. Whether you're working on a big project or just want to streamline your workflow, you'll learn how to use the advanced features in Excel and Google Spreadsheets. By the end of this chapter, you'll be able to take your spreadsheet skills to the next level and impress your colleagues.

I. Advanced Formulas and Functions

Using conditional formulas

Conditional formulas allow you to perform different calculations based on the value of a cell or range. For example, you can use the IF function to perform different calculations based on whether a cell contains a number greater than or less than a certain value.

Using array formulas

Array formulas allow you to perform calculations on a range of cells. For example, you can use the SUMIFS function to sum all of the values in a range of cells that meet certain criteria.

Using lookup and reference functions

Lookup and reference functions allow you to look up and reference data in other sheets or workbooks. For example, you can use the VLOOKUP function to look up a value in a table based on the value of a cell.

II. Advanced Formatting and Styling

Using styles and themes

Styles and themes allow you to quickly format and style your data. For example, you can use a style to format the text in a cell or range, or you can use a theme to change the colors and font of your data.

Using tables and pivot tables

Tables and pivot tables allow you to organize and analyze your data. For example, you can use a table to format your data, or you can use a pivot table to summarize and analyze your data.

III. Advanced Collaboration and Sharing

Using comments and notes

Comments and notes allow you to add comments and notes to your data. For example, you can use comments to add notes about your data, or you can use notes to add comments about your data.

Using track changes and versions

Track changes and versions allow you to track changes and versions of your data. For example, you can use track changes to track changes to your data, or you can use versions to view previous versions of your data.

By mastering these advanced tips and tricks, you'll be able to work more efficiently and effectively. You'll be able to take your spreadsheet skills to the next level and impress your colleagues. With the knowledge you've gained in this chapter, you'll be able to work like a pro.

Real-life Scenarios: Applying your skills in practice

In this chapter, we're going to take the skills and knowledge you've learned and apply them to real-life scenarios. We'll explore common tasks and challenges that you might encounter in the business world and show you how to use Excel and Google Spreadsheets to solve them. By the end of this chapter, you'll be able to apply your skills in practice and feel confident in your ability to use Excel and Google Spreadsheets at work.

I. Budgeting and Financial Analysis

Creating a budget

A budget is a financial plan that shows how much money you expect to earn and spend over a certain period of time. To create a budget in Excel or Google Spreadsheets, you can use a template or create your own. You'll need to input your income and expenses, and then use formulas and functions to calculate your total budget.

Analyzing financial data

Financial analysis involves examining financial data to understand trends and make predictions. To analyze financial data in Excel or Google Spreadsheets, you can use charts, pivot tables, and other tools to visualize your data and perform calculations.

II. Sales and Marketing Analysis

Analyzing sales data

Sales analysis involves examining sales data to understand trends and make predictions. To analyze sales data in Excel or Google Spreadsheets, you can use charts, pivot tables, and other tools to visualize your data and perform calculations.

Analyzing marketing data

Marketing analysis involves examining marketing data to understand trends and make predictions. To analyze marketing data in Excel or Google Spreadsheets, you can use charts, pivot tables, and other tools to visualize your data and perform calculations.

III. Human Resources and Operations Analysis

Analyzing employee data

Employee analysis involves examining employee data to understand trends and make predictions. To analyze employee data in Excel or Google Spreadsheets, you can use charts, pivot tables, and other tools to visualize your data and perform calculations.

Analyzing operational data

Operational analysis involves examining operational data to understand trends and make predictions. To analyze operational data in Excel or Google Spreadsheets, you can use charts, pivot tables, and other tools to visualize your data and perform calculations.

IV. Project Management

Tracking project progress

Project management involves creating a plan, monitoring progress, and making adjustments as needed. To track project progress in Excel or Google Spreadsheets, you can use Gantt charts, timelines, and other tools to visualize your progress and identify any issues or delays.

Managing tasks and deadlines

Managing tasks and deadlines involves creating a list of tasks, assigning them to team members, and setting deadlines. To manage tasks and deadlines in Excel or Google Spreadsheets, you can use task lists, calendars, and other tools to keep track of your progress and ensure that everything is on schedule.

V. Inventory Management

Tracking inventory levels

Inventory management involves keeping track of the stock of goods and materials. To track inventory levels in Excel or Google Spreadsheets, you can use inventory templates, charts, and other tools to visualize your data and perform calculations.

Managing purchase and sales orders

Managing purchase and sales orders involves creating and tracking orders for goods and materials. To manage purchase and sales orders in Excel or Google Spreadsheets, you can use templates, forms, and other tools to keep track of your orders and ensure that everything is running smoothly.

VI. CRM (Customer Relationship Management)

Tracking customer interactions

Customer Relationship Management (CRM) involves creating and maintaining relationships with customers. To track customer interactions in Excel or Google Spreadsheets, you can use templates, charts, and other tools to visualize your data and perform calculations.

Managing leads and opportunities

Managing leads and opportunities involves identifying and pursuing potential customers. To manage leads and opportunities in Excel or Google Spreadsheets, you can use templates, forms, and other tools to keep track of your leads and opportunities and ensure that you're following up with the right people at the right time.

VII. Social Media Management

Tracking social media metrics

Social media management involves creating and managing content on social media platforms. To track social media metrics in Excel or Google Spreadsheets, you can use templates, charts, and other tools to visualize your data and perform calculations. You can use these tools to track things like engagement, followers, and reach, and use the data to improve your social media strategy.

Managing social media campaigns

Managing social media campaigns involves creating and executing campaigns to promote your brand or products on social media. To manage social media campaigns in Excel or Google Spreadsheets, you can use templates, forms, and other tools to plan, execute and track the performance of your campaigns.

BOSSING SPREADSHEETS: A GIRL'S GUIDE TO DATA ANALYSIS

Girl, you've come so far! You've learned how to use Excel and Google Spreadsheets to solve real-life business scenarios like a boss. From budgeting and financial analysis to project management and social media management, you're now equipped with the skills and knowledge to take on any task that comes your way. And you know what the best part is? You're just getting started. With every day, you'll become more confident, more efficient and more powerful in using these tools.

Don't let anyone tell you that Excel and Google Spreadsheets are just for the boys, you're a girlboss and you're here to conquer the business world with data. You're going to walk into your next meeting and own it, you're going to make decisions based on data and not guesses. You're going to be the one everyone goes to when they need help with spreadsheets. You're going to be the one who's always ahead of the game, because you're a girl who's not just good with spreadsheets, you're a girl who's great with spreadsheets.

So, go out there and show the world what you're made of, girl! You got this!

Conclusion: Putting it All Together and Staying Ahead in Business

Congratulations, girl! You've officially completed the ultimate guide to mastering Excel and Google Spreadsheets. You've learned everything from the basics to advanced tips and tricks and you're now ready to tackle any task that comes your way. You're now a pro at data analysis, visualization, collaboration and automation.

But it's not just about the technical skills you've acquired, it's about the confidence and power you've gained. You're no longer intimidated by spreadsheets, you're in control. You've elevated your game in the business world and now you're ready to take on any challenge.

You're now equipped with the tools and knowledge to stay ahead in business, to make data-driven decisions, to streamline processes and to work smarter not harder. You're now a valuable asset in any team, any company, any industry.

But remember, learning doesn't stop here. Stay curious, stay hungry, stay ahead. Keep experimenting with new formulas, functions and features. Keep learning from others and sharing your knowledge. Keep pushing yourself to be the best version of yourself.

And always remember, you're not just a girl who's good with spreadsheets, you're a girl who's mastered them. You're not just good at business, you're great at it.

You got this!

Thank you for reading, and we hope you enjoyed the book and found it helpful. Remember to stay curious, stay hungry, stay ahead!